KINDERGARTEN MEASUREMENT AND DATA HANDLING

Fun-filled Activities

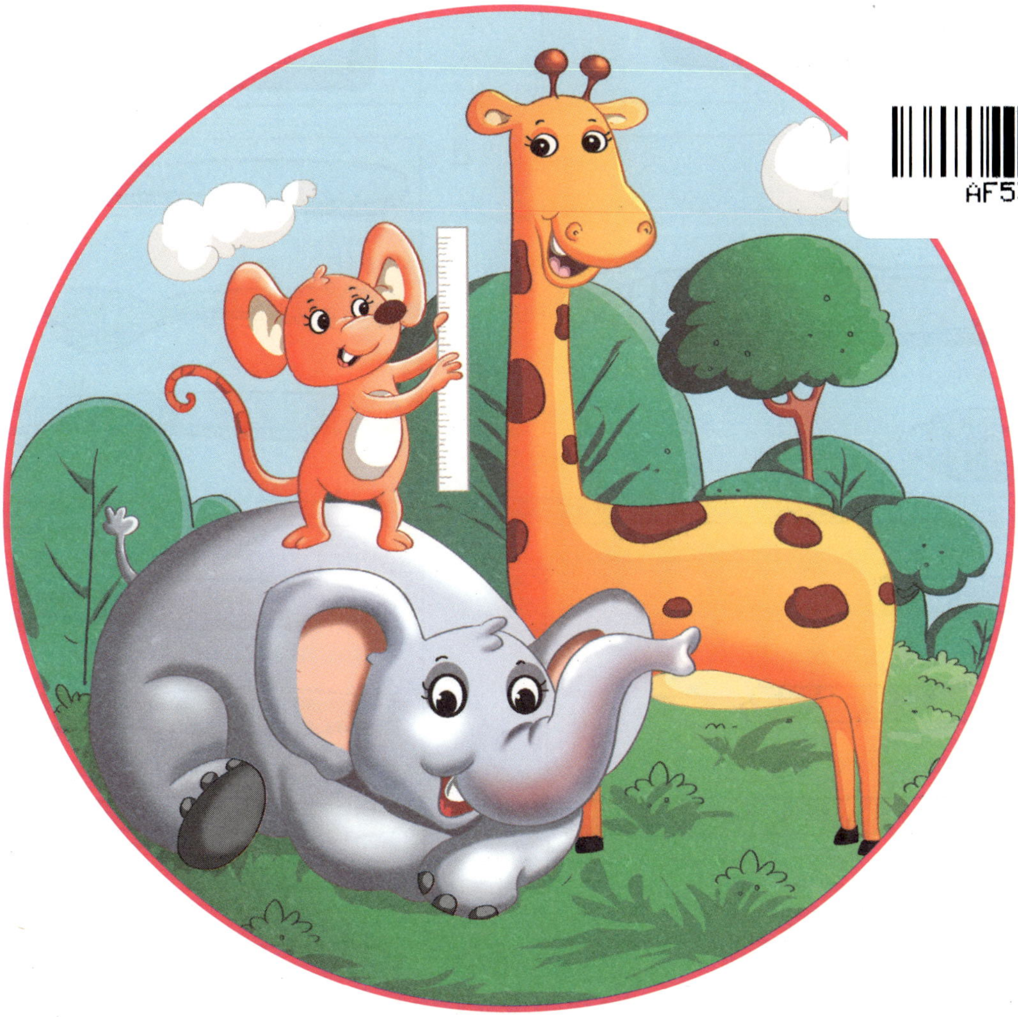

Om KIDZ
An imprint of Om Books International

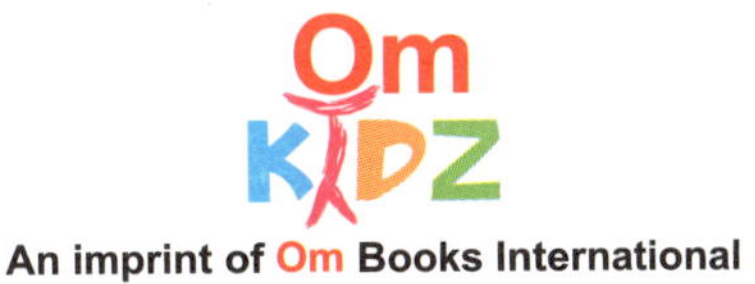

Longest And Shortest

In each box tick (✓) the longest picture and cross (×) the shortest one.

1.

2.

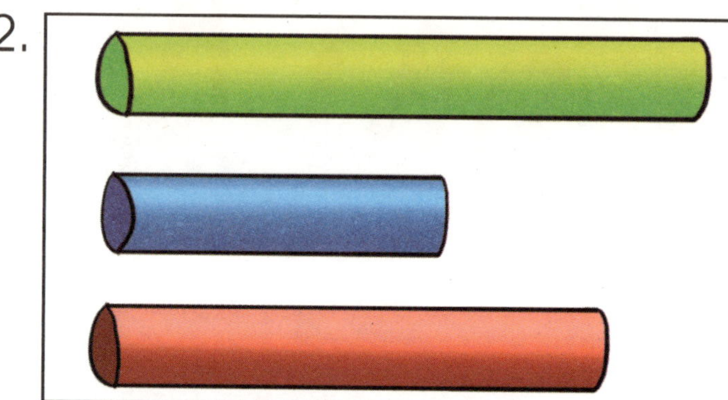

3.

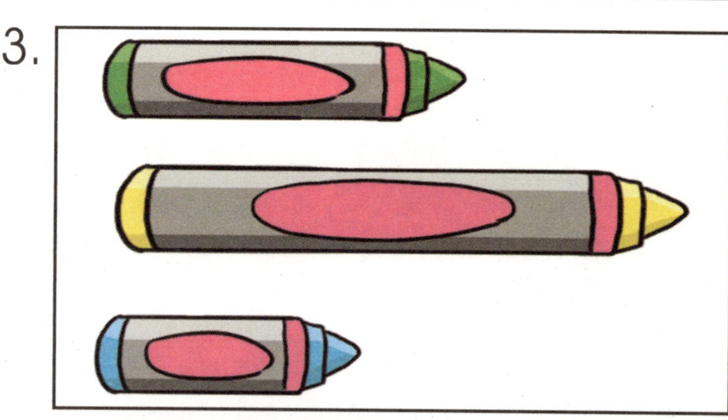

4.

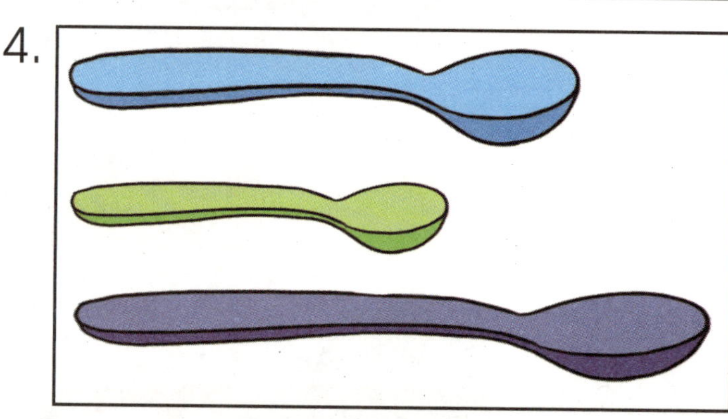

5.

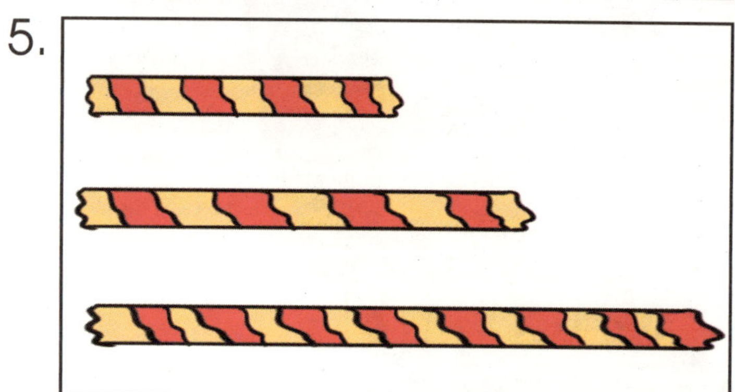

6.

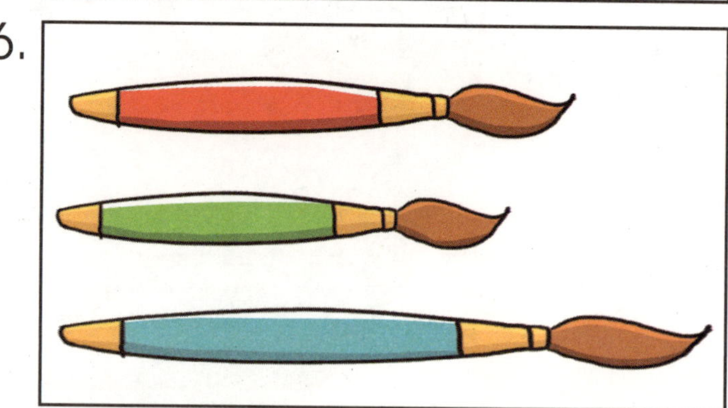

YOUR TURN

Draw 3 lines. Tick (✓) the longest and circle (O) the shortest.

Short To Long

Number the scarves in order 1, 2, 3, 4, 5 and 6 to show shortest to longest.

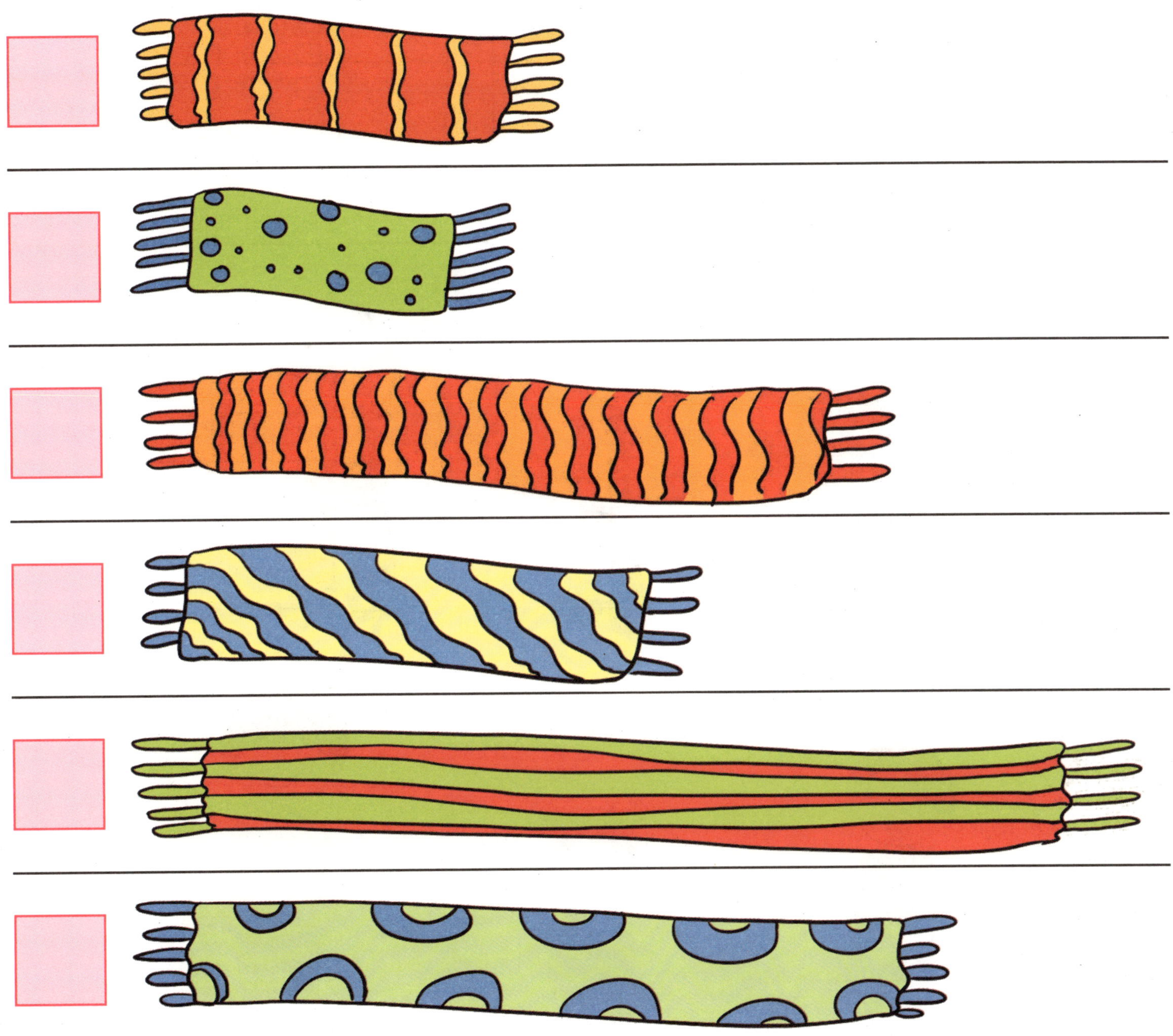

YOUR TURN

Draw 5 lines from shortest to longest. Circle (O) the line that is the longest.

Tallest And Shortest

Tallest Shortest

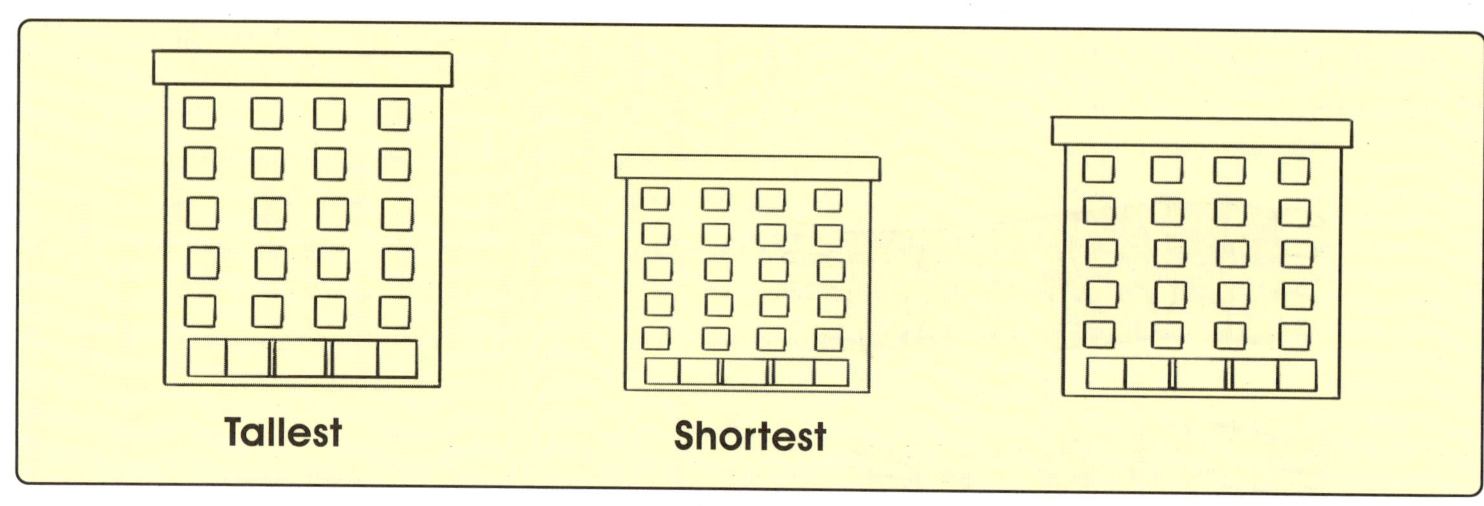

Circle (O) the tallest scarecrow with a .

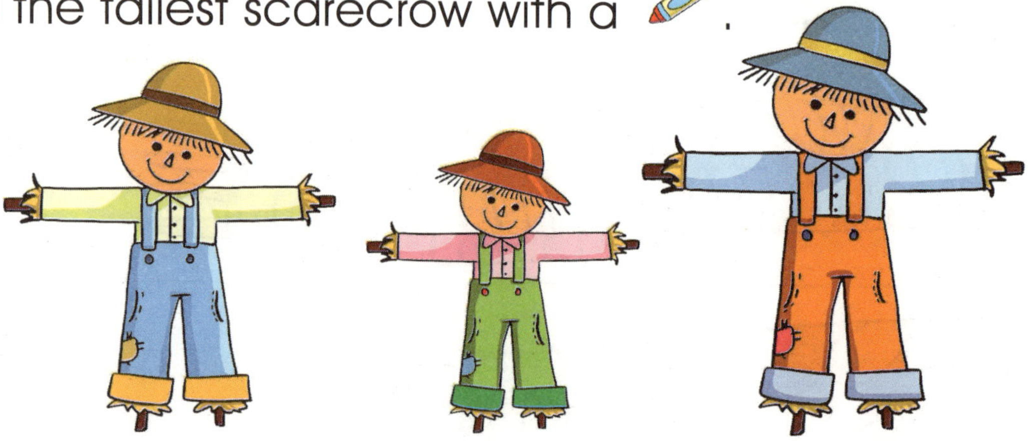

Tick (✓) the shortest child with a .

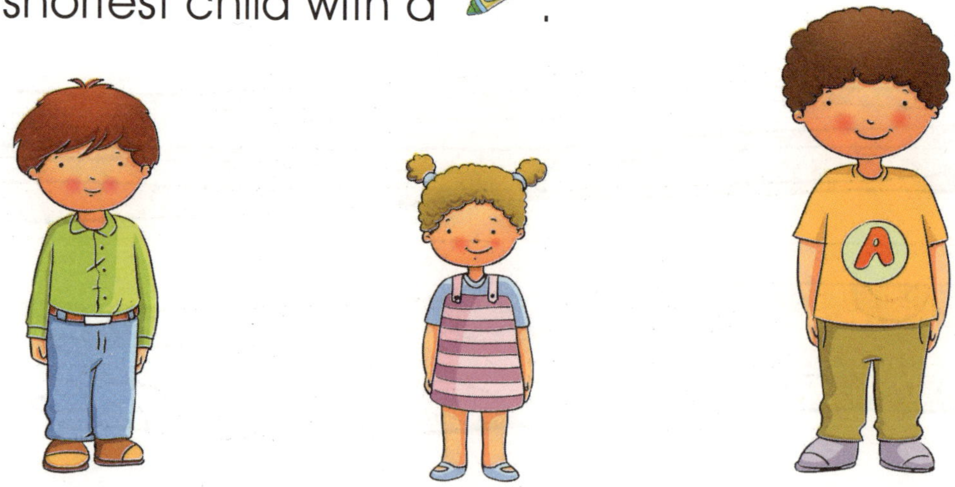

YOUR TURN

How tall are you? Have your mother/teacher measure your height against the wall and draw a mark.

Measuring Length In Units

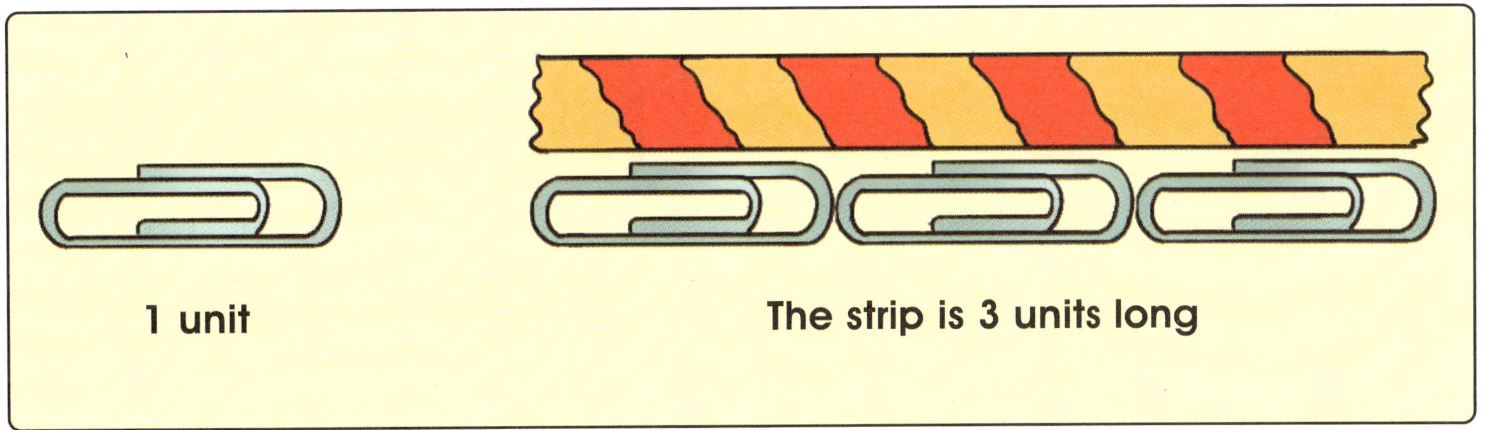

Write how many units.

______

______

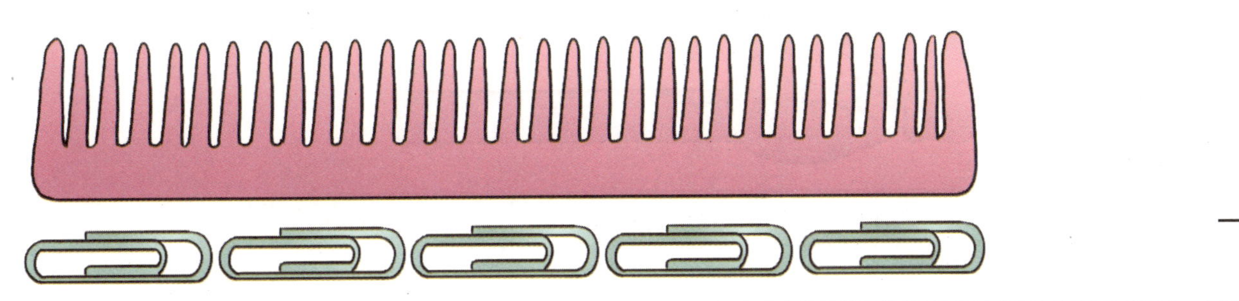

______

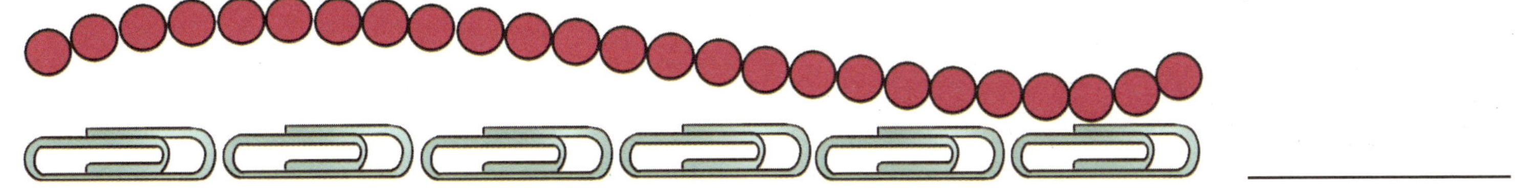

______

Measuring Length In Units

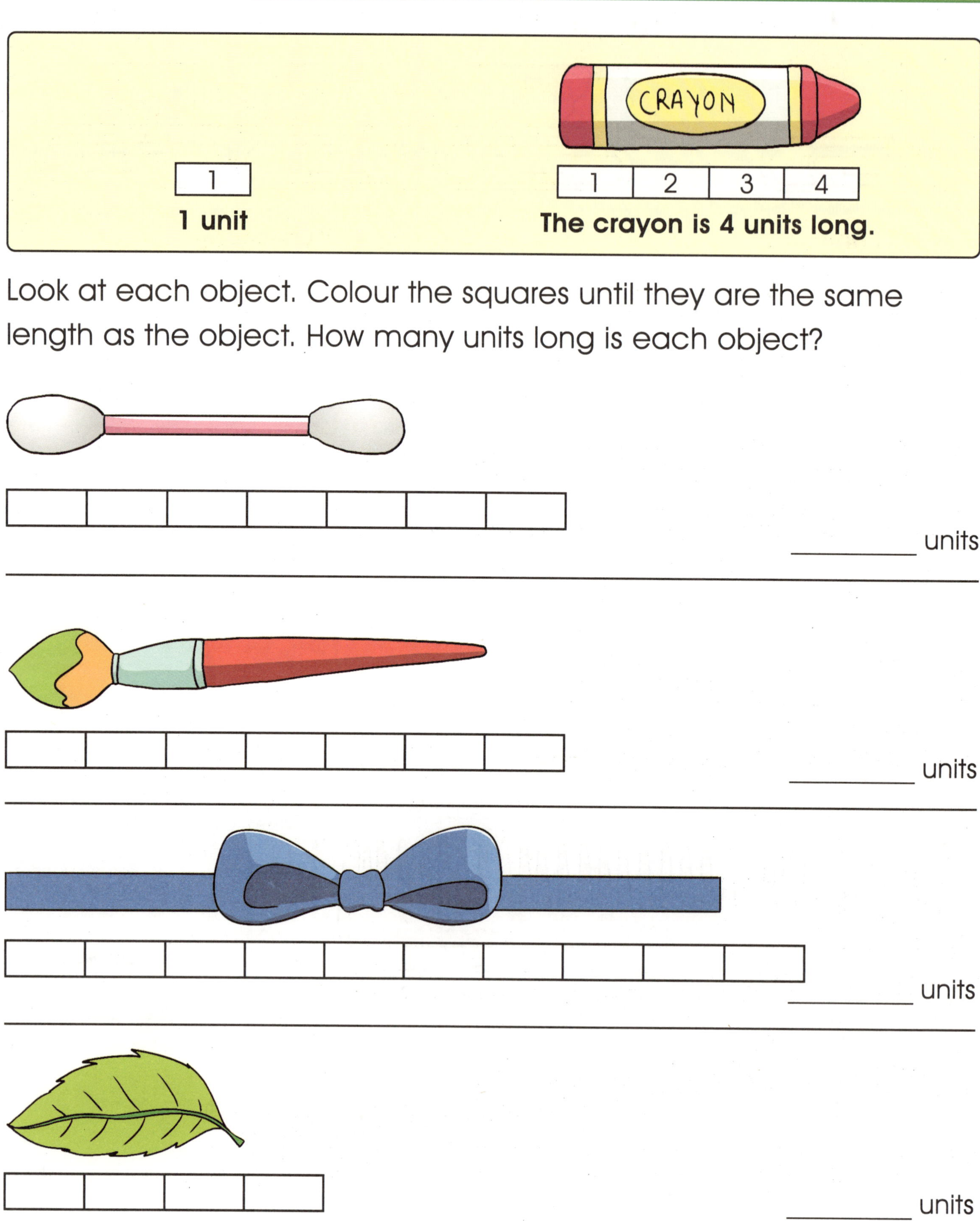

1 unit

The crayon is 4 units long.

Look at each object. Colour the squares until they are the same length as the object. How many units long is each object?

_______ units

_______ units

_______ units

_______ units

Heavier And Lighter

Look at each pair. Tick (✓) the lighter.

Heaviest and Lightest

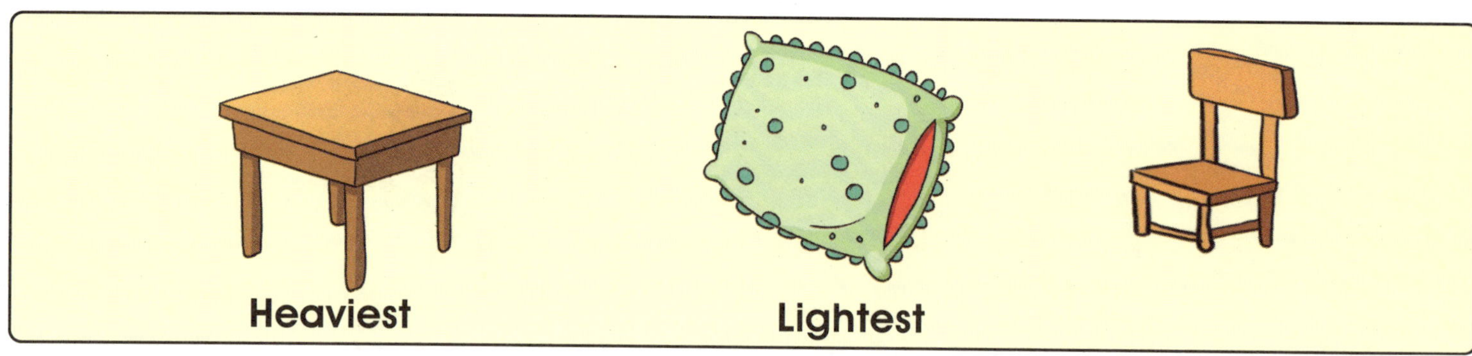

Circle (O) the heaviest in each row.

Circle (O) the lightest in each row.

YOUR TURN Find one object in the house that is heavier than you and one that is lighter. Name them.

Lightest To Heaviest

Number the pictures in order 1, 2, 3, 4, 5 and 6 to show lightest to heaviest.

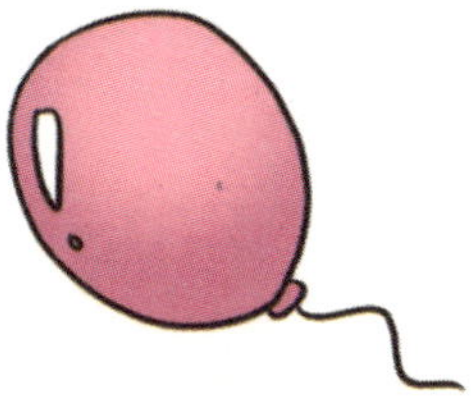

YOUR TURN

Draw 5 fish and number them 5 to 1 to show heaviest to lightest.

Let's Weigh

You need:

- an apple, a bottle full of water, a book, a milk carton, a pencil
- a rock to measure with

Do:

1. Use a balance scale.
2. Place the rock on one of the scales.
3. Place the other objects on the other scale one by one.
4. Compare which is heavier.
5. Line up the objects from lightest to heaviest.

Draw the objects here from lightest to heaviest.

Now draw the objects from heaviest to lightest.

YOUR TURN How did you know which one was heavier as compared to the rock?

Holds More Or Less

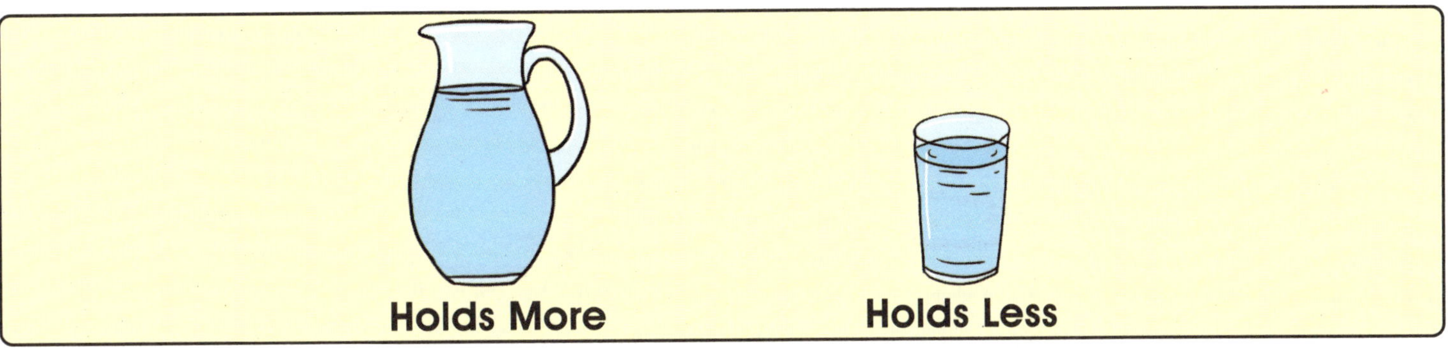

In each pair, circle (O) the one that holds **MORE**.

YOUR TURN Find two containers from the kitchen. Tell which one holds more.

Holds More Or Less

In each pair, circle (O) the one that holds **LESS**.

YOUR TURN

Molly has a jug.

Draw 2 containers for her such that:

- 1 should hold more than the jug.
- 1 should hold less than the jug.

How Much Fills?

You need:

- any two bottles or containers
- a cup to measure with
- water

Do:

1. Take two bottles or containers of different sizes.
2. Fill the first bottle with water using the cup.
3. Note how many cups were used to fill the first bottle.
4. Fill the second bottle with water using the cup.
5. Note how many cups were used to fill the second bottle.
6. Write the number of cups.

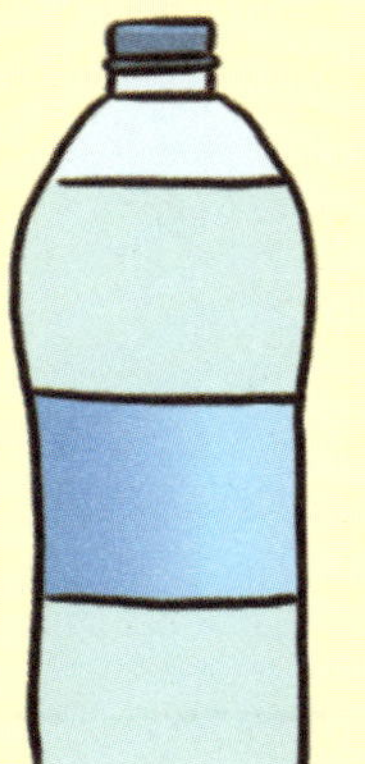

=  cups

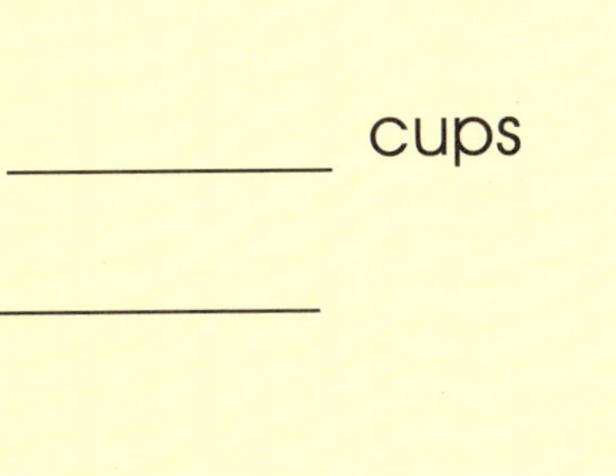

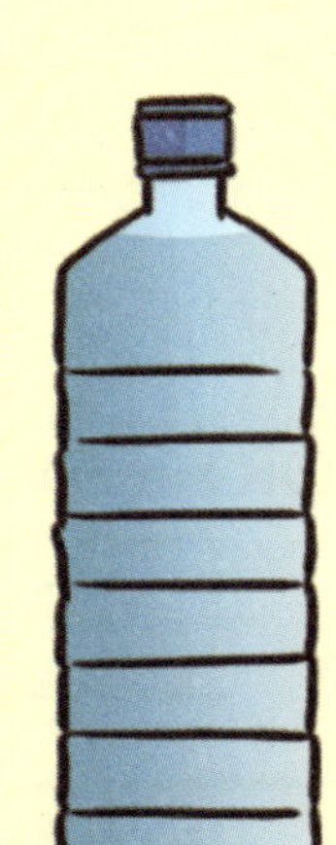

= ________ cups

____

7. Compare. Which bottle holds more water?
8. Write **holds more** and **holds less** for each.

Shape Express

Colour the shapes as per the colour codes.

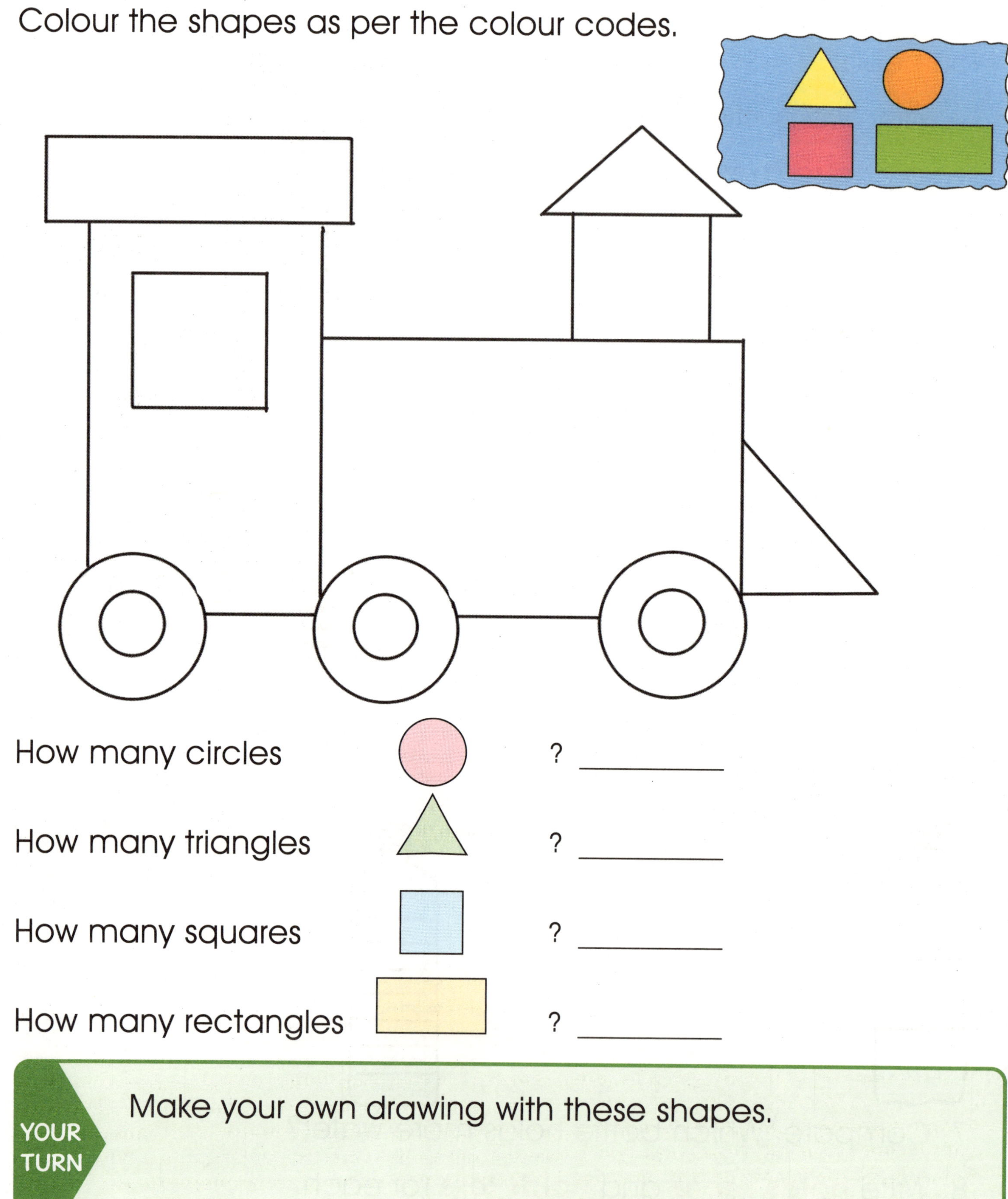

How many circles ? ________

How many triangles ? ________

How many squares ? ________

How many rectangles ? ________

YOUR TURN

Make your own drawing with these shapes.

Polly's Wall Hanging

Polly made a wall hanging using different shapes.

Write the total number of each shape.

Toy Tale

Jenny's toys are all messed up. Help her sort the toys according to the categories mentioned below.

How many toys have wheels? ________

How many toys are round? ________

How many toys have legs? ________

Other toys. ________

Walk, Fly Or Swim?

How many animals walk or run? ________

How many animals swim? ________

How many animals fly? ________

YOUR TURN

Are there any animals that can hop? How many? _______

At The Baker's

Pinto, the baker has a lot of items in his bakery. Count them and write the numbers.

Roll The Dice And Draw

Roll and throw the dice 4 times.

Draw balls to show your score.

1st throw

How many balls? ☐

2nd throw

How many balls? ☐

3rd throw

How many balls? ☐

4th throw

How many balls? ☐

YOUR TURN Count all the balls. Write how many are there in total. ☐

Alphabet Hunt

Jack has a bag full of letters.

Count and write how many of the following letters are there.

A – ☐

B – ☐

C – ☐

D – ☐

E – ☐

Which letters are missing in Jack's bag?

Draw And Circle

Draw the correct number of flowers on the stems.

Circle (O) the one with the most flowers.

3 flowers

5 flowers

4 flowers

7 flowers

My Fruit Basket

I want to collect fruits for my grandfather. Draw the fruits as per the numbers given.

YOUR TURN

How many fruits are there altogether?

Count And Make Tally Marks

Use the key to colour the pictures.

Count and write the number.

Make tally marks for each

Fly High

The birds are flying. Use the arrows as keys and colour the birds.

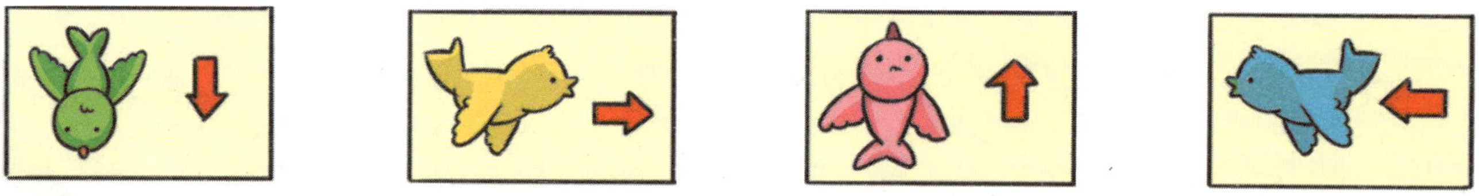

How many birds are flying UP ? ____

How many birds are flying RIGHT ? ____

Circle (O) the arrow which shows the birds that are MORE.

Flying LEFT  or DOWN 

Jenny's Pets

Look at the tally chart. Answer the questions.

Jenny's Pets		How many?
	𝍷𝍷𝍷	______
	𝍷	______
	𝍸𝍷	______

Which pet does Jenny have the most of? Circle (O).

Which pet does Jenny have the least of? Circle (O).

Winter Is Here

Find the similar objects and colour as many squares in the graph. Count how many are there of each.

Yummy Treat

Colour the same candies with the same colour.
Count them and colour the same number of boxes.

Which candy is the most in number? Draw here.

Which candy is the least in number? Draw here.

In The Sea!

Count the animals and write the number of each. Then, tally and graph.

Write the number

Tally here

Colour the same number of boxes as the number of animals.

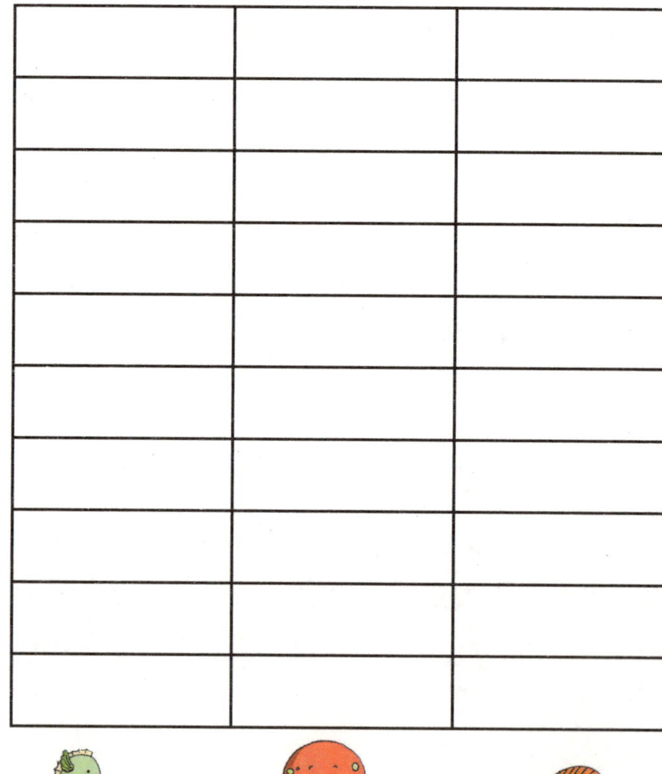

Draw the sea animal that is the most in number.

Letters In My Name

Write your name and the names of FOUR of your friends.

Write names here

1. ____________________
2. ____________________
3. ____________________
4. ____________________

Tick (✓) the letters that appear in the names.

A	B	C	D	E	F	G	H	I	J	K
L	M	N	O	P	Q	R	S	T	U	V
W	X	Y	V							

Count and write how many times each letter appears in all the names.

A – ☐
B – ☐
C – ☐
D – ☐
E – ☐
F – ☐
G – ☐
H – ☐
I – ☐
J – ☐
K – ☐
L – ☐
M – ☐
N – ☐
O – ☐
P – ☐
Q – ☐
R – ☐
S – ☐
T – ☐
U – ☐
V – ☐
W – ☐
X – ☐
Y – ☐
Z – ☐

Answer Key

Page 2

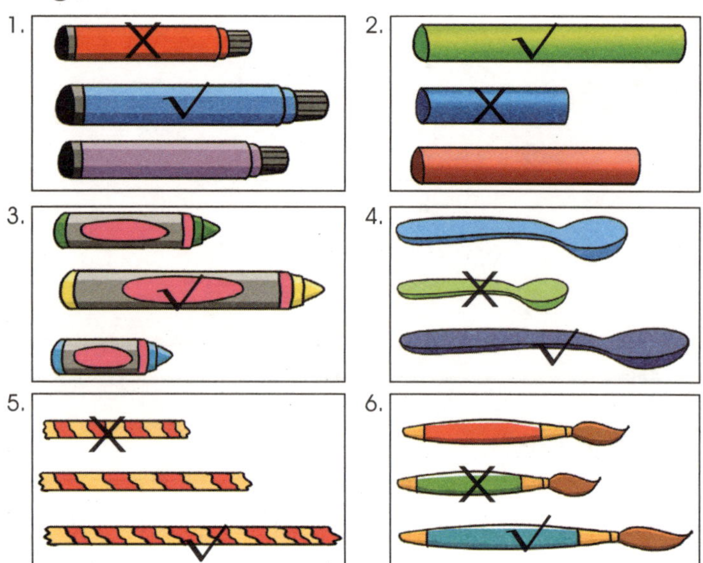

Page 3

The short to long order is – 2, 1, 4, 3, 6, 5

Page 4

Page 5

4 units

3 units

5 units

6 units

Page 6

5 units

6 units

9 units

3 units

Page 7

Page 8

Page 9

The correct order is – 6, 1, 4, 5, 3, 2

Answer Key

Page 10

Children will do with the help of parents.

Page 11

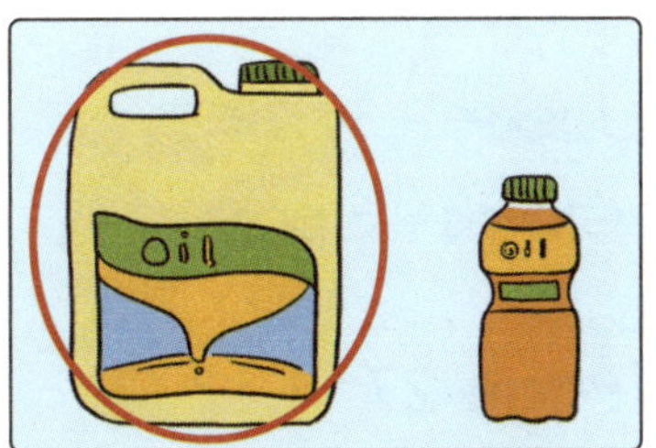

Page 12

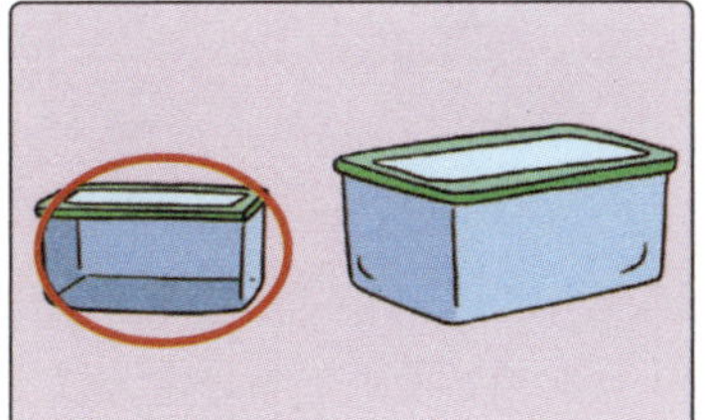

Page 13

Children will do with the help of parents.

Page 14

Children will do with the help of parents.

Circles – 6

Triangles – 2

Squares – 2

Rectangles – 3

Page 15

Spheres – 2

Cubes – 5

Stars – 7

Cones – 2

Page 16

Toys with wheels – 3

Round toys – 1

Toys with legs – 3

Other toys – 7

Page 17

Animals that walk or run – 5

Animals that swim – 3 (a frog can also swim)

Animals that fly – 3

Animals that can hop – 3

Page 18

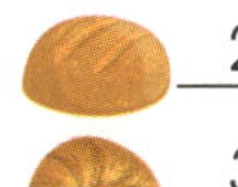 2

 2

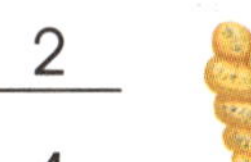 2

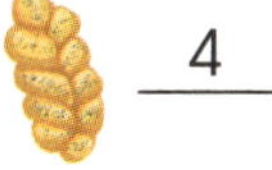 4

 3

 3

 4

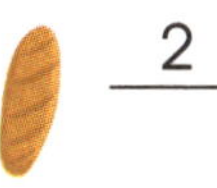 2

4

2

Page 19

Children will do with the help of their parents

Page 20

A – 5

B – 4

C – 2

D – 7

E – 2

Answer Key

Page 21
Children will do on their own.

Page 22
Children will do on their own.

Page 23

  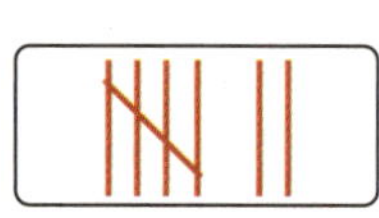

Children will make tally marks on their own.

Page 24

Birds flying up – 4

Birds flying right – 4

Birds that are flying left are more.

Page 25

Dogs – 3

Cats – 1

Fish – 6

Jenny has the most of fish and least of cats.

Page 26

Caps – 4

Boots – 3 pairs

Scarves – 5

Jacket – 3

Gloves – 3 pairs

Page 27

Children will do on their own.

Page 28

Children will do on their own.

Page 29

Children will do on their own.